The Book of
Truly Stupid
Sports
Quotes

THE BOOK OF
TRULY STUPID
SPORTS
QUOTES

JEFF PARIETTI

HarperPerennial
A Division of HarperCollinsPublishers

HarperCollins books may be purchased for educational, business, or sales promotional use. For information, please write to: Special Markets Department, HarperCollins Publishers, Inc., 10 East 53rd Street, New York, New York 10022.

FIRST EDITION

Designed by Nina Gaskin

Library of Congress Cataloging-in-Publication Data

Parietti, Jeff.
    The book of truly stupid sports quotes / Jeff Parietti. — 1st ed.
      p. cm.
    ISBN 0–06–273408–3
    1. Sports—Quotations, maxims, etc.   2. Athletes—Quotations.
  3. Sports—Humor. I. Title.
  GV706.8.P37 1995
  796'.0207—dc20
                                            95-46840
                                            CIP

96 97 98 99 00 ❖/HC 10 9 8 7 6 5 4 3 2 1

CONTENTS

PREFACE

It's a challenging endeavor to put together a collection of quotes that will tickle the ol' funny bone.

Of course, that challenge is made easier by focusing on the sports world. Nowhere else can there be found such an amusing variety of funny, witty, sarcastic and just plain truly stupid quotes.

This book represents the best material selected from several thousand quotes collected during an intensive research process.

Inside are quotes from just about anyone associated with sports, including players, coaches, owners, officials and announcers.

To maintain the original essense of each quotation, team affiliations are listed as of the time the individual made the comment.

Compiling this book has been quite an adventure of both hard work and enjoyment. Thanks to my family, relatives and friends for their words of support and encouragement. It's that type of caring that helps an author to maintain the determination, discipline and persistence necessary for achieving the final goal of a published work.

Also, a special thanks to Rob Kaplan at HarperCollins for his able assistance and belief in this project.

Finally, thanks to you, the reader. May this book offer you many hours of laughter and enjoyment!

Jeff Parietti
April 1996

Chapter 1

NO BRAINERS

"I'm in the best shape of my life and that includes my brain."

—Lenny Dykstra, Philadelphia Phillies outfielder

"Our goal is to get him through one game without having to use his batting helmet in the outfield."

—Manager Nick Leyva on Wes Chamberlain, Phillies rookie outfielder

"Why does everybody stand up and sing 'Take Me Out to the Ballgame' when they're already there?"

—Larry Andersen, major league hurler

"That's so when I forget how to spell my name, I can still find my clothes."

—Stu Grimson, Chicago Blackhawks left wing, explaining why he keeps a color photo of himself above his locker

"Physically, he's a world-beater. Mentally, he's an eggbeater."

—Michigan center Matt Elliott, describing Ohio State linebacker Alonzo Spellman

"If you put his brain in a blue jay, it [the bird] would fly backwards."

—Chicago Cubs hurler Al Nipper on pitcher Mitch Williams

"He's missing something upstairs, but that's what makes him a player."

—Tony Phillips, California Angels utility man,
about teammate Rex Hudler

"I asked the doctor before he closed the wound if he could put some brains in there."

—Outfielder Rex Hudler, after smacking into a wall
while trying to snare a foul ball

"If it's your brain, you'll be fine. That's the smallest organ in your body."

—Charles Barkley to Golden State Warrior Chris Mullin, who had fainted

"They keep me pretty much in the dark about everything. If it had blown up, I wouldn't have known anything about it."

—Dennis "Oil Can" Boyd, Boston pitcher, after the Red Sox didn't inform him about a bomb threat against a team flight

"I know the Virginia players are smart because you need a 1500 SAT score to get in. I have to drop bread crumbs to get our players to and from classes."

—George Raveling, Washington State basketball coach

"I play football. I'm not trying to be a professor. The tests don't seem to make sense to me, measuring your brain on stuff I haven't been through in school."

—Clemson recruit Ray Forsythe, who was ineligible as a freshman because of academic requirements

"Why would anyone expect him to come out smarter? He went to prison for three years, not Princeton."

—Boxing promoter Dan Duva on Mike Tyson hooking up again with promoter Don King

"Sometimes, God gives you physical talent and takes away the brain."

—Mike Ditka, Chicago Bears coach, on the crowd-inciting antics of Green Bay Packer linebacker Tim Harris

"The problem is, I don't know any exercises for their brains."

—Glen Sather, Edmonton Oilers coach, trying to correct his team's defensive flaws

"I get on my horse and go out and stand in the middle of the woods and listen to birds. That's how I am. Sometimes I go out in the woods and, you know, maybe talk to a tree."

—Kirk Gibson, major league ballplayer, on his relaxation techniques

"To be honest, I don't think we have any brains out here."

—Ken Green, when asked which PGA Tour player would win a "Jeopardy" game

"I'm not sure when I'm going to play again. I've had enough brain damage for August."

—Nick Faldo, after an 8-over 80 at the PGA championship

Chapter 2

OH, REALLY!

"Most of my clichés aren't original."

—Chuck Knox, Los Angeles Rams coach

"It was a little different. It was like playing inside."

—Steve Webber, University of Georgia baseball coach, after a game in the Superdome

"I don't want to get into that, but Mike's got a whole new set of bannisters."

—Don King on Mike Tyson's "lawyer" situation

"Tonight, we're honoring one of the all-time greats in baseball, Stan Musial. He's immoral."

—Johnny Logan, ex–major leaguer, introducing Musial
at a banquet

"The world will end before there is another .400 hitter . . . I think that was mentioned in the Bible."

—Lenny Dykstra, Philadelphia Phillies outfielder

"It isn't like I came down from Mount Sinai with the tabloids."

—Ron Meyer, Indianapolis Colts coach, downplaying his decision to start rookie quarterback Jeff George

"That picture was taken out of context."

—Jeff Innis, New York Mets pitcher, griping about his bad newspaper photo

"All of his saves have come during relief appearances."

—Ralph Kiner, New York Mets broadcaster, on reliever Steve Bedrosian

"He's a great player. He ceases to amaze me every day."

—Ray Perkins, Tampa Bay Buccaneers coach, on kicker Gary Anderson

"His reputation preceded him before he got here."

—Don Mattingly, New York Yankee first baseman, about playing against the Mets' Dwight Gooden in an exhibition contest

"We figured if we shut them out, there's no way we can lose."

—Brett Wallerstedt, Arizona State linebacker, after 19–0 victory over Louisville

"They didn't outplay us."

—Darryl Major, Missouri linebacker,
on a 73–0 loss to Texas A&M

"We certainly played with a lot of intensity. The score is certainly no indication of the way Fisher [High] played."

—Girls' hoop coach DoBee Plaisance, St. Martin Episcopal
in New Orleans, on squad's 72–0 win

"Our record may lead everyone to think that we are just a ridiculously sorry team, but we're not."

—Vincent Brown, New England Patriots linebacker, downplaying the team's 1–9 mark

"We have lost a couple of games at home which we probably wouldn't have lost a couple of years ago, and not because of the talent level, just because of the inexperience of the building."

—Jerry Krause, Chicago Bulls general manager, about the team's new United Center

"He [Julio Cesar Chavez] speaks English, Spanish, and he's bilingual, too."

—Don King, boxing promoter

"Before, I couldn't make any important putts. Now I miss more than I did, but I also make more than I did."

—Mike Hulbert on making the switch to putting with just his right hand

"Defensively, I think it's important for us to tackle."

—Karl Mecklenburg, Denver Broncos linebacker,
assessing team's strategy for trying to beat
the San Francisco 49ers in Super Bowl XXIV

"I didn't think there were too many problems other than two interceptions in the red zone and one blocked field goal."

—49ers quarterback Steve Young after a 10–7 loss to Houston

"I don't care what anyone says, Navy will be the surprise team in the country."

—Lou Holtz rating the Midshipmen, coming off a 1–10 record the previous season

"I don't think anywhere is there a symbiotic relationship between caddie and player like there is in golf."

—Johnny Miller, TV analyst and pro golfer

"If we're going to run away from Toronto, first we've got to catch them and go by them."

—Mike Stanley, New York Yankees catcher

"I think we're capable of going exactly as far as we go."

—Chris Ford, Boston Celtics coach, forecasting his team's chances in the playoffs

"I'll be sad to go, and I wouldn't be sad to go. It wouldn't upset me to leave St. Louis, but it would upset me to leave St. Louis. It's hard to explain. You'll find out one of these days, but maybe you never will."

—Brett Hull, St. Louis Blues right wing, on a possible trade

Chapter 3

GEOGRAPHY LESSONS

**"Hawaii doesn't win many games
in the United States."**

—Lee Corso, football television analyst, trying to explain
the Rainbows' poor mainland record

**"All of the Mets' road wins against
Los Angeles this year have been at
Dodger Stadium."**

—Ralph Kiner, New York Mets broadcaster

"The only thing I know about it is that it's in New Jersey."

—Michael Crouwel, Dutch catching prospect, asked about Philadelphia after being obtained by the Phillies

"Great! That's the Italian city with the guys in the boats, right?"

—Murad Muhammad, boxing promoter, on a possible Venezuela fight

"The sky is so clear today you can see all the way to Missouri."

—Sportscaster Jerry Coleman,
calling a Royals game in Kansas City, Missouri

"This is the first time I've ever played in the United States. I've played in Montreal, Venezuela, Japan, and Alaska."

—Warren Cromartie, Kansas City Royals first baseman

"I've played in Japan.
Is that anywhere near Asia?"

—Golfer Fred Couples, asked if he ever played a round in Asia

"I was in the dark. I actually thought
it was below California, not above."

—Cliff Robinson, Portland Trail Blazers rookie,
about his new team's location

"We got to see all of Hearne, and parts of His'n."

—Shelby Metcalf, Texas A&M hoop coach, after a snowstorm stranded the team in the small Texas town of Hearne

"The way I've been going, I couldn't drive Miss Daisy home."

—Andy Van Slyke, Pittsburgh Pirates outfielder, on his RBI slump

"I mostly stayed around the house. But I did take a hunting trip to one of those Canadian proverbs."

—Jim Gantner, Milwaukee Brewers infielder, describing his offseason activities

"He once asked me if Beirut was named after that famous baseball player who hit home runs."

—Brother Ray Page, St. Anthony High School teacher in Jersey City, on alumnus Bobby Hurley of the Sacramento Kings

"Shaq's house is in such a great neighborhood [that] the bird feeders have salad bars and the Salvation Army has a string section."

—Pat Williams, Orlando Magic general manager

"I don't know. I've never played there."

—Golfer Sandy Lyle on his opinion of Tiger Woods

"People asked me if I was going to a Halloween party last fall. I told them 'Who needs Halloween when you spend time in Berkeley?'"

—Reggie Jackson

"They boo for a living in those places. We played on Christmas Eve and they even booed Santa Claus."

—Jerry Glanville, Houston Oilers coach, on Cleveland and Cincinnati fans

"He wasn't supposed to hit it over there."

—Roberto Kelly, New York Yankee left fielder, after failing to chase Brewer George Canale's fly-ball double down the line

"I ain't been nowhere, but I'm back."

—Rocky Lockridge, journeyman boxer

Chapter 4

DUMB AND DUMBER

"I quit school in the sixth grade because of pneumonia. Not because I had it, but because I couldn't spell it."

—Boxer Rocky Graziano

"It took me five years to learn to spell Chattanooga—and then we moved to Albuquerque."

—Joe Morrison, South Carolina grid coach, about his earlier coaching stops

"I don't think there are going to be that many people writing books this year. We don't have that many people who can read and write."

—Cornerback Mark Collins, comparing the New York Giants' Super Bowl XXI and XXV championship squads

"But the real tragedy was that 15 hadn't been colored yet."

—Florida coach Steve Spurrier, after a blaze burned 20 books at Auburn's football dormitory

"I gave Gary a hockey puck once, and he spent the rest of the day trying to open it."

—Pat Williams, Orlando Magic general manager, assessing NBA executive Gary Bettman's chances of becoming NHL president

"You guys line up alphabetically by height."

—Bill Peterson, Florida State football coach

"Tell Len I'm very proud of him. I hope he does better next time."

—Toki Lockhart, after her grandson, Len Barker, tossed a perfect game

"I thought in overtime you get another foul."

—John Lucas, Philadelphia 76ers coach, upon attempting to send a fouled-out Shawn Bradley back into the game

"That doesn't bother me, but it did upset me when the principal said it was a rather stupid class overall."

—Lou Holtz on placing 234th of 278 in his high school class

"The Indians don't pay me to think. Computer analysts think. Stockbrokers think. Baseball players do not."

—Mel Hall, Cleveland Indians outfielder, asked for his thoughts about being shifted to center

"They told me to hit. Nobody said anything about running."

—Jimmy Key, Toronto Blue Jays pitcher, out at first on a ball hit to right field during an exhibition contest

"They're not the smartest people in the world. They have a diamond diagramming where they have to go. And they still have coaches on first and third telling them which way to go. Otherwise, these guys would run all the way to the warning track."

—Benny Ricardo, ex-NFL kicker turned comedian,
on baseball players

**"That's what I get for thinking
on a baseball field."**

—Cleveland Indians outfielder Albert Belle, off to the minors
for not running out a double-play grounder because
he thought there were two outs

"I've had teams before that if you told them to 'go back door,' they left the gym."

—Jim Valvano, North Carolina State hoop coach

"You mean we got to go with people?"

—Willie Wilson, Oakland outfielder, informed that the A's were taking a commercial flight instead of a charter

"Play some Picasso."

—Chris Morris, New Jersey Nets forward, making an unusual musical request to a piano player in a hotel bar

"Great, isn't it? I've got a $2,000 computer and all I know how to do is play the golf game on it."

—Mark Hardy, New York Rangers defenseman

"I don't really hate rookies, I just wish they were smarter."

—Don Nelson, Golden State Warriors coach

"She says, 'Dad, I got you the lead in a movie . . . *Dumb and Dumber, Part II*. You're going to get to play both parts.'"

—Tom Asbury, Kansas State basketball coach, on his daughter's comments after he called TCU coach Billy Tubbs a jerk and an idiot

Chapter 5

MUST BE SOMEONE ELSE

"Nobody in football should be called a genius. A genius is a guy like Norman Einstein."

—Joe Theismann, football television commentator
and ex-NFL quarterback

"Unfortunately, in society you tend to learn more by mistakes and by failure than you do by positives. With the mistakes I've made, I'll probably be Einstein pretty soon."

—Dave Brown, New York Giants quarterback

"I'm often mentioned in the same sentence as Michael Jordan. You know, 'That Scott Hastings, he's no Michael Jordan.'"

—Scott Hastings, NBA journeyman center

"'Marvelous Marvin' and 'Sugar Ray': Sounds like a pillow fight between a hairdresser and an interior decorator."

—Comedian Jan Murray before the Hagler-Leonard bout

"I heard Tonya Harding is calling herself
the Charles Barkley of figure skating.
I was going to sue her for defamation
of character, but then I realized I have
no character."

—Charles Barkley

"I usually don't give a good first
impression—or a good second impression.
For that matter, I usually come across like a
sack of manure."

—Doug Rader, Texas Rangers rookie manager

"Picture a barnyard full of pigs at the trough."

—Mike Brown, Cincinnati Bengals general manager, describing agents

"When a big senior calls you 'Boxhead,' you like it."

—Joel "Boxhead" Porter, Baylor offensive tackle, on why he accepted that nickname as a freshman

"They told us that we are pioneers for the World League, so you can just call me 'Lewis and Clark.'"

—Big offensive lineman Caesar Randle, a first-round pick in World League of American Football draft

"What do you think I am, a geologist?"

—Bill Peterson, Florida State coach, asked if he thought rain
would fall before a big football game

"When my wife was sick, I took care of her.
I was a regular Florence Nightinguy."

—Yogi Berra

"And at second base, it's Mickey Moriano."

—Ralph Kiner, New York Mets broadcaster, combining
Philadelphia's second-base platoon of Mickey Morandini and
Mariano Duncan

"What was he doing with Miss Saigon?"

—Buck Showalter, New York Yankees manager, upon hearing
that general manager Gene Michael had gone to see the
Broadway play *Miss Saigon*

"You go beyond the hair, tattoos, and the earrings, and he's like you and I."

—San Antonio Spurs coach Bob Hill on Dennis Rodman

"Does that mean I have to play Hamlet?"

—Ron Guidry, New York Yankees pitcher, told that he would be filling a lot of "roles" during the season

"He looks like a guy who went to a fantasy camp and decided to stay."

—Don Sutton, Atlanta Braves broadcaster, on roly-poly John Kruk

"We played about as soft as you can play. We played like a bunch of marshmallows."

—Jerry Sloan, Utah Jazz coach, after losing to the inept Los Angeles Clippers

"I went through life as a player to be named later."

—Joe Garagiola

"Maybe he can help us."

—Billy Connors, New York Yankees pitching coach,
after hearing that Cameroon had shut out
Argentina in World Cup soccer

Chapter 6

FASHION STATEMENTS

"I lost 15 pounds, so I look darn good in my tutu."

—Seattle Mariners pitcher Keith Comstock, who took offseason ballet classes to strengthen his back

"I'd rather have something for around $300 from a sheep that fooled around a little."

—Chuck Daly, Detroit Pistons coach, passing on a $1,300 virgin wool suit

**"He's one man who didn't let success
go to his clothes."**

—Mike Ditka on John Madden

**"I'd change hairdressers. Wing tips are
supposed to be for your shoes,
not the top of your head."**

—Chicago Bears quarterback Jim McMahon on what he would
change if he were coach Mike Ditka

**"He treats us like men. He lets us wear
earrings."**

—Torrin Polk, University of Houston receiver, about Cougars'
coach John Jenkins

"This ring may end up in a gutter. But if it does, I'll be wearing it."

—Mark Moseley, Washington Redskins kicker, upon getting his Super Bowl ring in 1983

"He's so hot he must be wearing asbestos shorts."

—Nick Faldo about Fred Couples' hot streak on the links

"The only reason he got that underwear commercial instead of me is because he likes to wear pink underwear."

—Phoenix Suns guard Dan Majerle roasting quarterback Boomer Esiason at a charity event

"The reason women don't play football is because 11 off them would never wear the same outfit in public."

—Comedienne Phyllis Diller

"[We] should be allowed to wear shorts. Gaudalmighty, women are allowed to wear 'em [on the LPGA Tour], and we've got better legs than they do."

—Greg Norman after a round in nearly 100-degree heat

"It's hard to find heels that don't have Mickey Mouse on them."

—Gymnast Brandy Johnson, on trying to find size-3 shoes

Chapter 7

NAKED NONSENSE

"When I was in the majors, I worked on a nudist ball. It had nothing on it."

—Phil Hennigan, ex–Cleveland Indians hurler

"I think we probably expose our players to the media as well as anybody."

—George Perles, Michigan State football coach, on allowing female sportswriters in the locker room

"Don't know. They were wearing a bag over their head."

—Yogi Berra, asked if a "streaker" was male or female

**"In the hunt to buy the
San Francisco Giants was George Shinn,
owner of the Charlotte Harlots."**

—Ralph Kiner, New York Mets announcer

**"It would take some of the lust off
the All-Star game."**

—Pete Rose on the possibility of interleague play

"Somebody asked me if I'm going to dress for the game. I said no, I'm going out there naked to prove a point. The point? That I'm not dressed."

—Matt Millen, Washington Redskins linebacker

"In the original Olympics, they competed completely naked. That'll cut down on your product endorsements."

—Comedian Dennis Miller

Chapter 8

BODILY FUNCTIONS

"We'll be back with the recrap after this message."

—Ralph Kiner, New York Mets broadcaster

"Some guy wanted me to run on a treadmill, with bottles hooked up to my arms. They were going to put it in perfume and call it 'Essence of Shaq.'"

—Shaquille O'Neal on a commercial opportunity he rejected

"He goes off holding what looks to be a left leg."

—Broadcaster Phil Stone, as injured Texas A&M safety Steve Kenney left the field during a game with Stanford

**"His only limitation is his ability
to move around."**

—Joe Torre, St. Louis Cardinals manager,
assessing the outfield play of Pedro Guerrero

"When he sits down, his ears pop."

—Golden State Warriors coach Don Nelson on 7'6" center
Shawn Bradley

**"Billy was the only person I knew who
could hear someone giving him the finger."**

—Mickey Mantle on Billy Martin

"I couldn't hear Steve Young at the line of scrimmage. I snapped the ball when he goosed me."

—Jesse Sapolu, San Francisco 49ers center

"If you make one mistake, it can result in a vasectomy."

—Steeplechaser Mark Rowland, vividly describing why he thought his event is track and field's most dangerous

"My gluteus maximus is hurteus enormous."

—Tony Campbell, Minnesota Timberwolves forward, after falling hard on his hip

"If they feel good about how hard they work, and go in and throw up a little bit after the game, that's all I ask."

—Roger Reid, Brigham Young University hoop coach

"Oh, I can't do that. That's my bad side."

—Yogi Berra, after a photographer asked him to look straight at the camera

"Those people haven't seen the last of my face. If I go down, I'm going down standing up."

—Chuck Person, after his Indiana Pacers went down 2–0 to the Boston Celtics in the playoffs

"I was thinking about making a comeback, until I pulled a muscle vacuuming."

—Johnny Bench, after his career mark for home runs by a catcher was broken by Carlton Fisk

"I had nothing else to do."

—Atlanta Braves outfielder David Justice on his motivation for getting a nipple ring

"If you have something on your mind, call and get it off your chest."

—Gary Cruz, sports-talk radio show host

"Harmon [Killebrew] said never chew gum at the plate. It makes your eyeballs bounce up and down."

—Charles Mitchell, Cleveland Indians batting coach

"During the eye examination, the doc asked if he could read the bottom line. The Czech kicker said, 'Read it! I know him!'"

—Woody Hayes, Ohio State football coach, on recruiting a kicker from Czechoslovakia

**"I've always been quite an athlete
myself—big chest, hard stomach.
But that's all behind me now."**

—Bob Hope

**"Wherever I go, people are waving at me.
Maybe if I do a good job
they'll use all their fingers."**

—Frank King, 1988 Calgary Winter Olympics organizing
committee chairman, on his tough job

**"Maybe the fan was trying to tell me
I stink."**

—Neal Morton, University of Michigan basketball sub, after a
deodorant stick landed at his feet during a home game

**"It's not right to throw behind a guy.
Every player's got a big behind.
Shoot for that instead."**

—Terry Steinbach, Oakland A's catcher

"That's what I call the ultimate laxative."

—Otto Jelinek, Canada's Minister of Sports, after riding the luge
down the Calgary Winter Olympics course

Chapter 9

PLAYING BY THE RULES

"We're not attempting to circumcise rules."

—Bill Cowher, Pittsburgh Steelers coach

"Come on. I'm head of the chapel service this season. I'm not going to cheat."

—Kent Hrbek, arguing with umpire Vic Voltaggio

"What's the penalty for killing a photographer—one stroke or two?"

—Davis Love III, after his swing was affected by a camera going off

**"I'll take a two-shot penalty, but
I'll be damned if I'm going to play the ball
where it lies."**

—Elaine Johnson, pro golfer, after her tee shot bounced off a
tree and into her bra

**"I don't want to tell you any half-truths
unless they're completely accurate."**

—Dennis Rappaport, boxing manager

**"Each of us will be looking for an edge.
Do they make corked fishing poles?"**

—Whitey Herzog on fellow baseball manager and angling buddy
Davey Johnson

"The U.S. Congress can declare war with a simple majority, but we need a three-fourths majority to go to the john."

—Cleveland Browns owner Art Modell describing a typical NFL owners' meeting

"If Dick Butkus was a cab driver and he had Ray Charles in the back seat, he'd rev up the engine for 50 minutes and charge him full fare."

—Benny Ricardo, ex-NFL kicker

"Someday they'll have offsetting 15-yard dance penalties."

—Atlanta Falcons coach Jerry Glanville on a new NFL rule forbidding on-field celebrations

"It's nice to see it's legitimate again after all those steroid and point-shaving scandals of the past."

—Sportscaster Bob Costas on the chance that ballroom dancing may become an Olympic sport

"That's what I get for kicking Sans in his face."

—American Mike Evans, after his ejection for kicking Spain's Jordi Sans in the face during a water polo game

**"We've got to find a way to win.
I'm willing to start cheating."**

—Tight end Marv Cook of the 0–6 New England Patriots

**"He made a stupid call and it will be stupid
till the day he dies. He's stupid Hank. That's
his nickname. It was a bogus call and he did
a stupid thing. But we're all human."**

—Charles Barkley, after being ejected by
referee Hank Armstrong

**"I'm not worried about taunting rules
because I don't taunt to nobody."**

—John Starks, New York Knicks guard

**"It's this kind of game that makes you wish
there was an 'uncle' rule in the NFL."**

—Broadcaster Merlin Olsen during Denver's 41–14
rout of Seattle

Chapter 10

IT'S ALL RELATIVE

"I have a God-given talent . . . I got it from my dad."

—Julian Winfield, Missouri basketball forward

"Buy one and send it to my mother. It's her fault I look like this."

—Don Zimmer, Chicago Cubs manager, on looking like an old bulldog in a newspaper photo

"I blame my dad now. He didn't work with me enough on the pass rush at a young age."

—Mike Golic, Philadelphia Eagles defensive end, on having no quarterback sacks well into one season

"I don't care if my mother's out on the field. I'm going to smack her and take her face off and then apologize after the game."

—Don Conley, Syracuse linebacker

"This one person called and said, 'You're nothing but a spoiled, greedy brat who has been spoiled your entire life.' I finally had to say, 'Mom, calm down.'"

—Keith Comstock, Seattle Mariners relief pitcher, on crank calls he received during a baseball lockout

"My mom was real happy. She was elated at everything, too."

—Steve Karsay, Toronto Blue Jays' first pick in amateur draft

"It's a marriage. If I had to choose between my wife and my putter, well, I'd miss her."

—Gary Player on his 26-year old putter

"Yeah, but I love you more than football and basketball."

—Manager Tommy Lasorda to his wife, who declared that he loved baseball and the Dodgers more than her

"My wife got tired of sharing me with another woman."

—Cleveland Indians outfielder Mel Hall on why he retired
"Lucille," his 11-year-old glove

"I'd have two wives. You can get away with it out there."

—Robert Parish, Boston Celtics center, on what he'd do if
traded to the Utah Jazz

"That's our mother-in-law set—constant nagging and harassment."

—Rick Pitino, Kentucky basketball coach,
describing one of his pet defenses

**"If he raced his pregnant wife,
he'd finish third."**

—Tommy Lasorda on former Dodgers catcher Mike Scioscia

**"That putt was go good, I could feel the
baby applauding."**

—Pregnant Donna Horton-White after sinking a 25-foot putt in
an LPGA tourney

"When [my wife Ann] presented me with our first child, I said, 'This is our cheerleader.' As our sons came after that I said, 'This is our quarterback, this is our center,' and so on. When the sixth child came, Ann said, 'This is the end.'"

—Bobby Bowden, Florida State football coach

"Scott Bullett, as he takes left field, is getting congratulations from everybody. He and his daughter are parents now of a new baby."

—Harry Caray, Chicago Cubs broadcaster

"Well, that lot's full. Let's see if I can park this baby someplace else."

—JoAnne Carner, after smacking her first two tee shots into a parking lot

"He's just perfect for mounting."

—Mike Hulbert, pro golfer and avid fisherman, on the birth of his 8-pound, 3-ounce son

**"He struck out three times and lost one
game when a ball went through his legs.
Parents swore at us and threw things at our
car as we left the parking lot. Gosh, I was
proud! A chip off the old block."**

—Bob Uecker, about one of his son's memorable
Little League experiences

**"My kids didn't see it,
so I didn't set a bad example."**

—Jim Bowden, Cincinnati general manager, on shoving his foot
through the family television set during a Reds' loss

"Wow, you can be in both clubhouses at once!"

—Jim Gantner, Milwaukee Brewers coach, upon meeting a reporter's twin brother

"Buddy was like my favorite uncle. The one I wanted to tell, 'Shut up.'"

—Gary Fencik, ex–Chicago Bears defensive back, on Buddy Ryan

"Three of my wives were very good housekeepers. After we got divorced, they kept the house."

—Willie Pep, ex-featherweight champ,
who was married six times

"Ex-teams are like ex-wives. Deep, deep down, you know you can't stand them."

—Charles Barkley on why he wanted to beat his old team,
the Philadelpia 76ers, by 100 points

Chapter 11

WATER WORLD

"He's a lifeguard in the offseason. He can't swim, but he's great at wading."

—Pat Williams, Orlando Magic general manager,
on 7'6" Shawn Bradley

"The old one didn't float too well."

—Craig Stadler on why he was using a
new putter at the U.S. Open

"He can hit just as good right-handed as he can left-handed. He's just naturally amphibious."

—Yogi Berra on Mickey Mantle

"You know what they do when the game is rained out? They go to the airport and boo bad landings."

—Bob Uecker on Philadelphia Phillies fans

**"We'll jump off that bridge when
we come to it."**

—Coach Jack Ramsay, when it was suggested that
his Buffalo Braves were headed toward one of the
NBA's worst-ever season records

**"We're going to be exciting. . . . Of course,
it was exciting when
the *Titanic* went down."**

—Bobby Weiss, Atlanta Hawks coach

"When everybody bowed at once, it looked like a giant Wave."

—Hakeem Olajuwon on his pilgrimage to Mecca

"The center's rear-end was all sweaty."

—Kyle Morris, Florida Gators quarterback, on why the ball kept slipping out of his hands

"Showers."

—Oakland A's manager Tony La Russa, after asking reliever Dennis Eckersley if he had heard the forecast

Chapter 12

EATING & DRINKING

"His idea of a salad is putting a piece of lettuce on a pizza."

—Pat Williams, Orlando Magic president, on 300-pound-plus center Stanley Roberts

"Depends on how far my refrigerator is."

—George Foreman, asked about how far he runs in training

"He thinks a triple-double is three double-cheeseburgers."

—Ray Kist, Niagara University basketball team trainer, on an overweight student manager

"I'm on such a strict diet, I don't even listen to dinner music."

—Bill Kofender, ex-publicist for the Detroit Race Course

"We'll be back after this word from Manufacturers Hangover."

—Ralph Kiner, New York Mets announcer

"I told the caddie I wanted a sand wedge and he brought me a ham on rye."

—Chi Chi Rodriguez

**"My handicap is that I don't have
a big enough beer cooler for the back
of my golf cart."**

—Rick D'Amico, Houston Gamblers linebacker

**"You can't even jump high enough to touch
the rim, unless they put a Big Mac on it."**

—Charles Barkley to 300-pound teammate Oliver Miller

"You can come and run the Boston Marathon and pass out, and we will get you moving to the beer party in 35 minutes."

—Dr. William Castelli, who gives IVs to dehydrated runners

"He tells me to drink lemon juice after a hot bath, but I can never finish the bath."

—Bob Uecker on his doctor's advice for getting rid of a cold

"We started him eating the seven basic food groups, and now there are only three left."

—Pat Williams about working with Stanley Roberts on his diet

"It's not like you're getting them out of a tavern somewhere. Okay, we got some out of a tavern."

—John Robinson, Los Angeles Rams coach, discussing replacement player quality during 1987 NFL strike

"You know it's summertime at Candlestick when the fog rolls in, the wind kicks up, and you see the center fielder slicing open a caribou to survive the ninth inning."

—Comedian Bob Sarlatte

"What's the big deal? I was hungry, man. It's not like I committed a crime."

—Willie Burton, Miami Heat guard, after he ordered and ate a pizza on the bench while sidelined with an injury

"He can be a great player in this league for a long time if he learns to say two words: 'I'm full.'"

—Atlanta Falcons coach Jerry Glanville on Lincoln Kennedy, 300-pound rookie offensive lineman

"I never got full. But I got tired of chewing."

—Steve Hyche, Arizona Cardinals linebacker, on devouring five steaks daily to gain 26 pounds during the offseason

**"If Stanford is a No. 12 seed, then I'm
a left-handed ham sandwich."**

—Wimp Sanderson, Alabama basketball coach, on NCAA
tourney seeding

"No, I'm a vegetarian."

—Wali Muhammad, cruiserweight boxer, on whether he had bit
opponent James Salerno

Chapter 13

MOUTHY HAPPENINGS

"I don't want to shoot my mouth in my foot, but those are games we can win."

—Sherman Douglas, Boston Celtics guard,
on upcoming schedule

"I don't like tobacco because it causes diseases. Dirt is free, and no one bums it off you."

—Todd Welborn, New York Mets' minor league reliever,
on why he chews dirt

"My mouth has never felt so soothed and relaxed."

—Chris Garway, Canadian World University Games
competitor, after mistaking mentholatum pain rub
for toothpaste

**"Now you see guys kissing. Man, I tell you,
it would be a cold day in hell before I would
kiss somebody on the other team."**

—Kevin McHale on the NBA's buddy-buddy atmosphere

"I love Charles [Barkley] because he's so honest. You can see a thought form in his head and then come right out his mouth without stopping in between."

—Boston Coach Chris Ford

"We're experiencing audio difficulties."

—Ralph Kiner, New York Mets broadcaster

"I'm just lucky I was wearing a mouthpiece. If I hadn't been, I would be using those teeth to play backgammon."

—Rony Seikaly, Miami Heat center,
after catching an errant elbow

"Yeah, I spit tonight. Hey, we're not going to the prom."

—Pittsburgh Pirates manager Jim Leyland on his failure
to quit chewing tobacco as evidenced by the
brown splotches on his white uniform

"He didn't know anything about drugs. He thought uppers were dentures."

—Archie Griffin, Ohio State running back,
on coach Woody Hayes

"If caring for a person is based on yelling and screaming, then he loves us very much."

—Terry Nelson, Cincinnati Bearcats forward,
describing coach Bob Huggins

"They feature a Buddy Ryan sandwich at his restaurant. It's a little tongue and a lot of baloney."

—Arnie Spanier, Phoenix sports-talk radio show host

Chapter 14

FAT TALES

"Now I look like a normal fat human being."

—Bubba Paris, San Francisco 49ers offensive tackle, describing his 340-pound physique after losing 40 pounds

"We were given a choice. We can either run around the field three times or around Tommy Lasorda once."

—Infielder Steve Sax on Los Angeles Dodger spring training workouts

"I don't know what all the commotion down there is, but it has somethin' to do with a fat lady."

—Dizzy Dean, St. Louis Browns announcer, as Queen of Netherlands was being seated

"He makes a great hitting background."

—Announcer Richie Asburn on 300-pound umpire John McSherry, positioned behind second base

"There have been a plethora of guys to hit it up there, but that was the plethorest."

—Chuck Pool, Florida Marlins publicist, after chubby Reds' outfielder Kevin Mitchell hit upper-deck homer at Joe Robbie Stadium

"In order to resemble William Perry, we have rented a Winnebago for our offensive line to practice against."

—Duke coach Steve Sloan preparing for Clemson's 320-pound nose guard

"The competition level is tremendous. It isn't like high school, where some fat guy's going to guard you."

—Guard Johnny Dawkins, comparing the NBA and amateur ranks

"I don't know what he has. A pulled groin. A hip flexor. I don't know. A pulled something. I never pulled anything. You can't pull fat."

—Bruce Coslet, New York Jets coach, on a player's injury

"Like they say, it ain't over till the fat guy swings."

—Darren Daulton, Philadelphia Phillies catcher, on stocky first baseman John Kruk

Chapter 15

THE ANIMAL KINGDOM

"In my next life, I want to come back as a kicker, or some fat lady's poodle. It's basically the same."

—Howie Long, Raider defensive end on kickers

"I ain't singing 'Happy Birthday' to no dog."

—Jim Leyland, spurning Marge Schott's party for her dog, Schottzie II, before a Pirates-Reds game

**"What's the difference between a
3-week-old puppy and a sportswriter?
In six weeks, the puppy stops whining."**

—Mike Ditka

**"I was trying to pull it back between barks,
but he got me on the backswing."**

—Lee Trevino, after missing a 3-foot putt due to a yapping dog

"It was just a little bit of animalistic barbarian verbiage."

—Brian Bosworth, Seattle Seahawks linebacker, explaining his on-field screaming outburst toward Denver quarterback John Elway

"I crashed in the chicken and broke the fingers of my feet."

—Raymond Roche, French motorcycle road racer, describing his crash in the chicane, which resulted in several broken toes

"They've got a broadcasters' wing and a players' wing. Maybe one day they'll have a chicken wing."

—"The Chicken," a.k.a. Ted Giannoulas, on his chance of making the Baseball Hall of Fame

"I'm so happy I could lay an egg."

—"Muddy," the Toledo Mud Hens mascot, after scratching out a shoe contract with a major manufacturer

"I'd like to apologize to the bird species for connecting these two."

—Mike Gottfried, Pittsburgh Panthers grid coach, who branded agents that prey on underclassmen as "vultures"

"I wonder if [Kevin] Bass is lonely now that Steve Trout is in the American League."

—Skip Caray, Atlanta Braves announcer

"Getting the fish through customs will be easy. The hard part was getting them to sit still for their visa pictures."

—Bob Walsh, Goodwill Games official, on shipping
Washington state trout to Moscow

"I guess you can say we added some Finns to the Sharks."

—Kevin Constantine, San Jose Sharks coach, after drafting five
players from Finland

"The skunk looked scared. I had just struck out. He was probably thinking, 'You stink worse than I do.'"

—First baseman Orestes Destrade, after an unwelcome smelly visitor dropped by the Florida Marlins dugout

"A lot of horses get distracted. It's just human nature."

—Nick Zito, trainer of 1994 Kentucky Derby victor Go for Gin

"He's probably the most famous person in northern California."

—John Growney, owner of Pro Rodeo Hall of Fame bull Red Rock from Red Bluff

Chapter 16

HAIRY MOMENTS

"You know that isn't really his hair. They found that hanging off some horse's butt."

—Jerry Glanville on the dreadlocks of San Francisco 49er
tight end Jamie Williams

"He doesn't cut that hair. He mows it."

—Chick Hearn on Dennis Rodman's green hairdo

"If he wanted me to run 26 miles through hills, I would. If he wanted me to carry water bottles, I would. If he wanted me to get my hair cut like his . . . well, you have to draw the line somewhere."

—Babe Laufenberg, ex-Dallas Cowboys backup quarterback, on Jimmy Johnson

"On the mound is Randy Jones, the left-hander with a Karl Marx hairdo."

—Broadcaster Jerry Coleman

"In Cincinnati, we were lucky to have eyebrows."

—Dann Bilardello, former Red, on the team's overly strict edicts regarding facial hair

"Does that mean I have to shave my legs?"

—Andy Van Slyke, Baltimore outfielder, on Orioles' policy of no hair below the lip

"He'll never be broke because Texaco just bought the rights to his head and they're going to start drilling next week."

—Banquet emcee Jerry Farber on coach Pat Riley's slicked-back hairstyle

"When the sportswriters describing it as salt-and-pepper dropped the pepper."

—Del Harris, Los Angeles Lakers coach, on when he realized his hair had become completely white

"It's the hair."

—Pat Leahy, veteran New York Jets placekicker, disagreeing that athletes' legs are the first thing to go

Chapter 17

HEAD CASES

**"That wasn't lotion on his head.
That was turtle wax."**

—Joe Kleine, Phoenix Suns center,
on Charles Barkley's bald noggin

**"I went to see him about three times, and
then he went to see a psychiatrist."**

—Mitch "Wild Thing" Williams, describing the impact he made
on his hypnotherapist

**"The shoulder surgery was a success,
the lobotomy failed."**

—Mike Ditka on quarterback Jim McMahon's surgery

**"We all get heavier as we get older because
there's a lot more information in our heads.
Our heads weigh more."**

—Vlade Divac, Los Angeles Lakers center

"If he gets you in trouble, and you see three bald heads, aim at the middle one."

—Archie Moore's advice to James "Quick" Tillis before bout
with Ernie Shavers

"The problem is in my head, because I shoot free throws well in practice."

—Wilt Chamberlain, explaining his difficulties
at the charity stripe

**"My head feels different after practice
than it did when I was a tailback.
It's like something is loose inside."**

—Terry Hollimon, Washington Husky,
after switching to linebacker

"It was so tight, I had trouble thinking."

—Danny Reed on helmet problems that made the 400-pounder
quit his Poca (W. Va.) High football squad

Chapter 18

NUMBSKULL NUMBERS

"If I've got anyone in there who doesn't realize we played a stinking game, then they've got Robert Parish's number [00] for an IQ."

—Coach Bill Fitch following his Los Angeles Clippers' 48-point loss to Portland

"This is his first major league debut."

—Steve Stone, Chicago Cubs announcer, on San Francisco Giants hurler Bill VanLandingham

**"I tried to make a one,
but I made two of them instead."**

—Al Kelley, PGA Senior Tour duffer,
explaining his 11 on one hole

**"The Phillies scored two runs in the fourth,
but the Braves countered
with one run in the second."**

—Announcer Jerry Coleman during a playoff game

**"You can sum up this sport in two words:
You never know."**

—Lou Duva, boxing trainer

**"You guys pair off in groups of three,
then line up in a circle."**

—Bill Peterson, Florida State grid coach

"We had lost four in a row, so it was very important to win this game. If we lose to Miami, it's like losing three games."

—Hakeem Olajuwon

"I was three-over—one over a house, one over a patio and one over a swimming pool."

—George Brett on his golf score

"Whenever I play with him, I usually try to make it a foursome—Ford, me, a paramedic, and a faith healer."

—Bob Hope on former President Gerald Ford

"Things could have easily gone the other way."

—Don Zimmer, Chicago manager, after Cubs' 4–4 road trip

"There's three things I hate about football, and they've got them all here: domed stadium, artificial turf, and the wave. They've got the quiniela here."

—John Madden, confusing a quiniela with a trifecta during a Seattle-Detroit game at the Kingdome

"I'm sorry I'm late. The President was calling me to congratulate me. He thought it was a five-game series."

—St. Louis Manager Whitey Herzog, jesting that Ronald Reagan had made him tardy for 1987 World Series postgame interview

"That play went 5–4–3 if you're scoring at home—or even if you're watching by yourself."

—ESPN's Keith Olbermann, describing a double play

"Jay Bell is 0 for 6 in the series with 10 homers and 52 RBIs."

—Ralph Kiner, New York Mets announcer

"Jose's trying to become baseball's first 40–40–40 player—40 homers, 40 stolen bases, 40 traffic tickets."

—Jim Lefebvre, Seattle Mariners manager, on Jose Canseco's traffic citations

"This fight is going to be 90 percent mental and 50 percent physical."

—Lou Duva, boxing manager

"Ninety percent of putts that are short don't go in."

—Yogi Berra

"Most football players are temperamental. That's 90 percent temper and 10 percent mental."

—Doug Plank, ex–Chicago Bears safety

"I can happily say I've made a 100-degree turn in my life."

—Boxer Hector Camacho on returning to the ring

"Any time Detroit scores more than 100 points and holds the other team below 100 points, they almost always win."

—Doug Collins, TV pro basketball analyst

"That was [Andy] Benes' fifth strikeout on the day. He came in with 94, so now he has 104 strikeouts on the year."

—Ralph Kiner

"I'm going to give 110 percent on every play. You can't give any more than that."

—Jimmy Johnson, University of Illinois quarterback

"Now that I'm here, we'll turn the program around 360 degrees."

—Jason Kidd, Dallas Mavericks' top draft pick

"The Mets just had their first .500 or better April since July of 1992."

—Ralph Kiner

**"This is one of the freakiest injuries
I've seen. And a bit annoying, because
I had to look up a number later."**

—John Adam, Milwaukee Brewers trainer, after pitcher Steve
Sparks dislocated his shoulder trying to rip a phone book in half

"Numbers on the guys' uniforms."

—Billy Joe Tolliver, San Diego Chargers quarterback, on what
he finds easiest to read on the defense

Chapter 19

HARD KNOCKS

**"I was trying to make friends,
but he's a hard guy to talk to.
I'm not fluent in cement."**

—Kelly Chase of the St. Louis Blues after a fight with
Chicago Blackhawk Wayne Van Dorp

**"I wanted to kill his body,
but he killed my face first."**

—Boxer Jimmy Bredahl on opponent Oscar De La Hoya

"I heard that Billy Buckner tried to commit suicide over the winter. He stepped in front of a car, but it went through his legs."

—Billy Gardner, Kansas City Royals manager, referring to infamous 1986 World Series miscue

"He takes a licking and keeps on ticking, like that Eveready bunny."

—Bill Cowher, Pittsburgh Steelers coach

"Andujar Cedeno to lead it off. He swings. And he is hit by a pitch. And it is hit over the wall and out of here for a home run."

—Ralph Kiner, New York Mets broadcaster

"When I went to Catholic High School in Philadelphia, we just had one coach for football and basketball. He took all of us who turned out and had us run through a forest. The ones who ran into the trees went on the football team."

—George Raveling, college basketball coach

**"'My goodness,' I thought,
'that's John Wayne. Why am I looking up
at him at this angle?' That's when I realized
I was on the canvas."**

—Boxer Floyd Patterson, after losing 1959 heavyweight title
bout to Ingemar Johansson

"My face is still standing, that's the key."

—Glen Featherstone, St. Louis Blues defenseman, on fight with
Minnesota North Stars tough Basil McRae

**"My nose didn't move.
It definitely had position."**

—Danny Schayes, Phoenix Suns center, after taking a nose shot
from Hakeem Olajuwon's elbow

**"If I stood there with frozen feet in front of
him, I wouldn't have time to be stupid,
because I'd be in a coma."**

—Roy Jones Jr., on how he might approach a bout
with George Foreman

"No more than usual."

—Boston Red Sox first baseman Dick Stuart, a.k.a. "Dr. Strangeglove," asked if he felt dizzy after being hit by a pitch

"I asked him to do some things that were difficult for him to do—like run back on defense, and pass."

—Don Nelson, Dream Team II coach, on Dominique Wilkins

"You have really solidified the Mets' center field problems."

—Announcer Ralph Kiner to outfielder Daryl Boston

"I think everybody gets caught up in superstitions. But I don't put much stock in them—knock on wood."

—Jim DeShaies, Minnesota Twins hurler

"I'm going to go out and putt on concrete for a while."

—Payne Stewart on preparations for the Augusta National greens at the Masters

Chapter 20

IDIOTIC SAYINGS

"Finish last in your league and they call you idiot. Finish last in medical school and they call you doctor."

—Abe Lemons, college basketball coach

**"Aw, don't worry about that, Doc.
If it happens, I could always come back
as a forward."**

—Harold Snepsts, St. Louis Blues defenseman, to a doctor who
advised him to wear a helmet to avoid brain damage

"You said run to the red light.
All the lights we saw were green."

—John-John Molina, junior lightweight boxer,
calling manager Lou Duva from a phone 10 miles from their
Virginia Beach, Va. hotel

"I'm an idiot—you can write that."

—Otto Baric, Austrian pro soccer coach suspended for spitting
at opposing players

**"Anybody who parked on the
railroad tracks, the Lincoln Police
Department wants you to move your car.
The university would like you to report
immediately for IQ testing."**

—Steve Johnson, P.A. announcer, during campus rally celebrating Nebraska Cornhuskers' football national title

**"I'm immature. I do everything
I can to stay stupid."**

—Bubba Baker, veteran NFL defensive tackle,
on why he still enjoys football

"The NFL, like life, is full of idiots."

—Randy Cross, football color commentator

"I'm not afraid to let people know that I'm kind of an idiot."

—Terry Bradshaw

"Not to listen to any radio sports-talk shows, because of all the idiots who call in."

—Mike Hargrove, Cleveland Indians manager, on what he learned from the previous season

"Show me an expert, and I'll show you an idiot."

—Sonny Hine, thoroughbred horse trainer

Chapter 21

TIMELESS THOUGHTS

**"A lot of people my age are dead
at the present time."**

—Casey Stengel, 72-year-old New York Mets manager

**"I told [Masters chairman] Hord Hardin I
was getting too old to play, but he kept say-
ing, 'Gene, they don't want to see you play;
they just want to see if you're still alive.'"**

—Gene Sarazen, 90-year-old Masters honorary starter

"When I broke in, we didn't have bats. We just grabbed a branch off a tree."

—Charlie Hough, Florida Marlins pitcher

"I've been here so long that when I got here, the Dead Sea wasn't even sick."

—Wimp Sanderson, University of Alabama basketball coach

"It went quickly, but it was like an eternity."

—Dave Winfield on spending nearly a decade with the New York Yankees

"If God had an agent, the world wouldn't be built yet. It'd only be about Thursday."

—Jerry Reynolds, Sacramento Kings executive

"Thank you, Don, you were on the floor longer than Fred Astaire in three of his movies."

—Comedian Alan King after a speech by boxing promoter Don King went into overtime

**"I'm going to graduate on time,
no matter how long it takes."**

—Rod Brookin, University of Pittsburgh senior basketball player

**"I'm really happy for Coach Cooper and the
guys who've been around here for six or
seven years, especially our seniors."**

—Bob Hoying, Ohio State quarterback,
after Buckeyes captured share of Big Ten title

**"The guy is 21 right now, and in 10 years,
he has a good chance to be 31."**

—Casey Stengel assessing a prospect's potential

"I'm between the twilight and the no-light of my career."

—Billy Olson, pole vaulter

"Then I was skinnier. I hit it better, I putted better, and I could see better. Other than that, everything is the same."

—Senior Tour player Homero Blancas, analyzing his golf game past and present

"I'm waiting for the Senile Seniors Tour."

—Bob Hope on his golf future

"It's when you start for home about the same time as you used to start for someplace else."

—Chris Dundee, boxing manager, explaining the meaning of time as one grows older

"Here's the man of the hour at this particular moment."

—Don King introducing victorious boxer Azumah Nelson

"I get up at 6:00 A.M. no matter what time it is."

—Yogi Berra

"I ain't doing nothin' and I don't do it before noon."

—Bum Phillips, ex-NFL coach

"Baryshnikov was great, but the play needs a shot clock."

—Bucky Waters, basketball analyst, after attending Broadway show "Metamorphosis"

"I left at halftime."

—Andre Agassi on his opinion of the musical "Les Miserables"

"There's always too much month at the end of the money."

—Maria Bottone on the hardships of training for the Olympic fencing squad

Chapter 22

FINANCIAL FOOLISHNESS

"People ask me why we didn't sign David Cone. Heck, we can't even afford an ice-cream cone."

—Jim Leyland, Pittsburgh Pirates manager

"Manute is so skinny, they save money on road trips—they just fax him from city to city."

—Woody Allen on 7'7" Manute Bol

"When George goes into a restaurant, he doesn't ask for a menu. He asks for an estimate."

—Lou Duva, boxing cornerman, on big George Foreman

"All I'm asking for is what I want."

—Rickey Henderson, Oakland Athletics outfielder, trying to renegotiate his meager $12 million, 4-year contract

"My best year was 1965, when I made about $21,000. And $17,000 of that came from selling other players' equipment."

—Bob Uecker

"He's the first guy to drive a $300,000 car with license plates he made himself."

—Jay Leno, after Mike Tyson bought four Bentley automobiles upon his release from prison

"I'd look for the guy who lost it, and if he were poor, I'd return it."

—Yogi Berra on what he'd do if he found $1 million

"I'm rich. What am I supposed to do, hide it?"

—Lou Whitaker, arriving in a stretch limousine for a players' union meeting during the 1994 baseball strike

"People would have to cut their lifestyle, and they'd live like penny-pinchers."

—Gary Payton, Seattle Sonics guard, about the hardships he claimed an NBA collective bargaining plan would have on players

"Potential is a French word that means,
'You aren't worth a damn yet.'"

—Jeff Van Note, Atlanta Falcons center

"I invited Bobby Knight over to my house
in San Juan and said, 'What's mine is yours.'
He sold it."

—Chi Chi Rodriquez

"We give all the players gas money, and we
give him covered wagon money."

—Doug Melvin, Baltimore Orioles official, on pitcher Daniel
Boone of AAA Rochester Red Wings

"It would be an honor to get something like that. . . . I have lots of trophies at home, but I bought them myself."

—Bert Blyleven on his chances for A.L. Comeback Player of the Year honors

"For a certain amount of money, you'll eat Alpo."

—Reggie Jackson on reports that he might sign to play baseball in Japan

"It must've had his contract in it."

—Dick Motta, Sacramento coach, after the Kings' Danny Ainge suffered a back injury while lifting his suitcase

"Ballplayers and deer hunters are alike. They both want the big bucks."

—Larry Doughty, Pittsburgh general manager, after a hunting trip with three Pirate players

"What do you have when you've got an agent buried up to his neck in the sand? Not enough sand."

—Pat Williams, Orlando Magic general manager

"It's a partial sellout."

—Skip Caray, Atlanta Braves broadcaster, on home-town "crowd" of 6,000 fans

"What the hell, she doesn't pay me, I pay her. Besides, what the hell position can a queen play?"

—Harold Ballard, Toronto owner, on why he had Queen Elizabeth's portrait removed from Maple Leaf Gardens

"I want to find out who this FICA guy is and how come he's taking so much of my money."

—Nick Kypreos, New York Rangers forward, preparing for team's White House visit after winning the Stanley Cup

"It was an insurance run, so I hit it to the Prudential Building."

—Reggie Jackson on his long homer at Fenway Park

"I'm independently wealthy. I have enough money to last me the rest of my life—provided I die tomorrow."

—Bill Fitch, NBA coach

Chapter 23

SLEEP AND DREAMS

"He used to have a bed check just for me every night. No problem. The bed was always there."

—Jim Rooker, ex-Pittsburgh Pirates pitcher,
on manager Chuck Tanner

"Every night I tell myself, 'I'm going to dream about my girl, I'm going to dream about my girl.' But it's always ham hocks."

—Nate Newton, 320-pound Dallas Cowboy guard

"I thought maybe I was going to become a general manager, because I kept wanting to take a nap."

—Jerry Glanville, Atlanta Falcons coach

"Tonight I'm going to sleep in my crouch."

—Sandy Alomar, after catching all 19 innings of a Cleveland Indians loss

"Every night when you lay your head on the pillow you say, 'I'm one of 300 [NBA players].' Of course, 50 of us stink really bad."

—Scott Hastings, journeyman center

"I couldn't sleep. I quit counting sheep and counted Cardinals."

—Joe Oliver, Cincinnati catcher, after he watched St. Louis score 28 runs against the Reds during a doubleheader

"If we lose I go home, crawl in bed, and suck my thumb."

—Buddy Ryan, Arizona Cardinals coach, on his postgame plans

"The fella is a bore. He could be at a party and no one would know he's there. He's a nice guy, but nice guys are only good at home. His poster could put people to sleep."

—George Foreman, discussing heavyweight boxer
Buster Douglas

**"I knew it was early because
Rocket Richard had his eyes closed in the
picture on the dressing room wall."**

—Vincent Damphousse, Montreal Canadiens forward,
on team's 6:00 A.M. practice session

**"He should have been better, pitching on
3,195 days rest."**

—Broadcaster Steve Blass on strike replacement player
Jimmy Boudreau, out of pro baseball for nearly nine years

"I was back in Jersey and I was waxing my car down. Then I thought I was dreaming that I was in a football game."

—Todd McNair, Kansas City Chiefs running back,
on his mild concussion from being sandwiched

"I watched the game and I got so scared I slept with the lights on all night."

—Buffalo Bills coach Marv Levy after viewing the
Raiders' Bo Jackson run right over Seahawks linebacker
Brian Bosworth, score three TDs, and rush for 221 yards

"I'd like to see the holes bigger."

—Fuzzy Zoeller, when asked about the changes
he would make in golf

"I love to wake up to garbage trucks
and gunshots."

—Diane Dixon, track star, on why she was returning to live
in Brooklyn after three years

Chapter 24

IT'S A TEAM GAME

"A lot of good ballgames on tomorrow, but we're going to be right here with the Cubs and the Mets."

—Thom Brennaman, Chicago Cubs broadcaster

"The last time the Cubs won a World Series was in 1908. The last time they were in one was 1945. Hey, any team can have a bad century."

—Tom Trebelhorn, Chicago Cubs manager

"Maybe you can talk the other team into throwing to you underhanded."

—A. J. Van Slyke, 7, offering some batting slump advice to his dad, Andy, of the Pittsburgh Pirates

"We were so bad last year, the cheerleaders stayed home and phoned in the cheers."

—Pat Williams, Orlando Magic general manager, on team's 1989–90 season

"Better teams win more often than the teams that are not so good."

—Tom Watt, Toronto Maple Leafs coach

"We're not stupid. We just play that way sometimes."

—Sam Wyche, Tampa Bay Buccaneers coach

"Even Jesus had trouble with 12 guys."

—Frank Layden, Utah Jazz general manager, on why the team
only had 11 players on its roster

**"In one of the greatest games in history—by
one team . . . "**

—Broadcaster Brent Musburger, after San Francisco 49ers'
55–10 Super Bowl XXIV rout of Denver

"We weren't even the second-best team out there."

—Bobby Weiss, Atlanta Hawks coach, after 35-point playoff loss to Chicago

"We're totally committed to defense. I'm not sure our defense is committed to defense, but the rest of our team is."

—Lou Holtz, Notre Dame coach

"We used to pray the White Sox and the Cubs would merge so Chicago would have only one bad team."

—Comedian Tom Dreesen on growing up
a baseball fan in Chicago

"We've got to be the worst 20–6 team ever."

—Perfectionist Pat Riley while coaching the Los Angeles Lakers

"That's the first time I've ever been beaten by a team that looked like it was trying to die."

—Coach Buddy Ryan on Arizona Cardinals' 14–12 loss
to the Los Angeles Rams

"If this keeps up, our team picture this year will be an X ray."

—Football coach John Cooper on Arizona State's many injuries

"I don't think there's anybody in this organization not focused on the 49ers . . . I mean Chargers."

—Bill Belichick, Cleveland Browns coach, slipping up before an upcoming game with San Diego

"We're kind of like a Fig Newton. We've got a soft cover and we're kind of gooey inside."

—Jerry Glanville, Atlanta Falcons coach

"We need more cohesion, rather than Stalinistic purges where you operate under a level of fear. We all need to join hands and sing 'Kumbaya.'"

—Brian Williams, Denver Nuggets

"They couldn't win with me and they couldn't win without me, so it must not have been me."

—Dominique Wilkins on the Atlanta Hawks, his former team

"No, we don't allow them to shoot. We spend almost no time working on shooting. We practice our entrance and exit to the locker room."

—Bobby Knight, asked if shooting would be a practice priority after Indiana's terrible game performance

Chapter 25

THANKS FOR THE MEMORIES

"I can't really remember the names of the clubs that we went to."

—Shaquille O'Neal, on whether he had visited the Parthenon during his trip to Greece

"I'll never forget my last time at the [Madison Square] Garden. Hundreds of people were screaming for me. I must have sold 250 hot dogs."

—Boxer Art Aragon

"Lay down so I can recognize you."

—Willie Pep, ex-featherweight champion, on seeing a former fighter whose name he didn't remember

"His nerves. His memory. And I can't remember the third thing."

—Lee Trevino on the three things that go as a golfer ages

"I used to have this slight speech implement and couldn't remember things before I took the Sam Carnegie course."

—Bill Peterson, Florida State football coach

"He's a quick learner, but he forgets quick too."

—Mychal Thompson, Los Angeles Lakers reserve center, on teammate Vlade Divac

"Hey, if I'm dumb enough to lose a piece of paper with $40,000 on a bar, do you think I can remember what year it was?"

—Roger Maltbie, about winning a golf tourney but misplacing the check

"Just remember the words of Patrick Henry—'Kill me or let me live.'"

—Bill Peterson on his halftime pep talk

"I don't know anything about Mantle or DiMaggio. Were they as good as Ken Griffey Jr?"

—Ruben Rivera, 21-year-old New York Yankee prospect, on being touted as the next Mickey Mantle or Joe DiMaggio

"This job is better than I could get if I used my college degree, which, at this point, I can't remember what it was in."

—Bob Golic, Raiders defensive tackle and Notre Dame graduate

**"I just walked off the field. I forgot
I was the coach."**

—June Jones, new Atlanta Falcons coach, on neglecting to meet
with the media following the opening day of minicamp

**"Back then, I got fined for breaking a
backboard. Nowadays, Shaq breaks a
backboard, and they make
a commercial out of it."**

—Darryl Dawkins, who shattered backboards 20 years ago

"I can't remember. I played 32 years without a helmet."

—Gordie Howe, on what happened the night he broke Maurice Richard's NHL all-time scoring record in 1960

"I'm the football coach around here and don't you remember it."

—Bill Peterson

Chapter 26

SIMPLEMINDED ODDS & ENDS

"Things are going so bad that I tried to stay at Motel 6 and they'd turned the light off."

—Kevin Hickey, major league reliever, on a bad streak

"[Rollie Massimino] had a great time and just raved about everything until the last day. Then he complained that the towels were so thick that he had a hard time closing his suitcase."

—Jim Valvano, recalling their trip to Italy

"Sure—I'm proud to be an American."

—Steve Foster, Cincinnati Reds rookie pitcher, asked by a Canadian customs agent if he anything to declare

"It's permanent, for now."

—Reds outfielder Roberto Kelly, announcing his switch to the name "Bobby"

"Mitch doesn't have ulcers. He's a carrier."

—Philadelphia Phillies manager Jim Fregosi on Mitch Williams

"Some guys are inwardly outgoing."

—Ralph Kiner, New York Mets announcer

"I am the best promoter in the world. And I say that humbly."

—Don King

"If only I had a little more humility, I would be perfect."

—Ted Turner, Atlanta Braves owner

"I feel like I'm the best, but you're not going to get me to say that."

—Jerry Rice, San Francisco 49ers receiver

**"If it's undisputed,
what's all the fighting about?"**

—Comedian George Carlin on the boxing term
"undisputed champion"

"No comment."

—Michael Jordan's reply on being named to
the NBA's all-interview team

"When coaches don't want to talk, they say you don't understand. It's funny how fans and media understand wins. But everyone gets stupid with losses. Losing breeds stupidity."

—John Madden

"It's irresponsible and shoddy journalism, but we're not going to react to it."

—John Maroon, Baltimore Orioles media relations director,
on a newspaper's spoof reporting
the end to Cal Ripken's ironman streak

"I don't pay any attention to those goons."

—Norman Braman, Philadelphia Eagles owner,
on sports-talk radio show hosts

"Fear was absolutely necessary. Without it, I would have been scared to death."

—Floyd Patterson, former heavyweight boxing champion

"A stiff is a guy without much talent, but who helps you win games. A guy without much talent who doesn't is a dog. A no-hoper is a guy who's not quite good enough to be a stiff yet."

—Doug Moe, Philadelphia 76ers coach

"If I dance after a home run, I don't think the pitchers would appreciate it. Baseball is a different game. In football, you're free to make a fool of yourself."

—Deion Sanders

"Thanks for not playing 'Jailhouse Rock.'"

—Pete Rose to Doc Severinsen after coming on "The Tonight Show Starring Johnny Carson."

"The greatest thing just happened. I got indicted into the Florida Sports Hall of Fame. They gave me a standing observation."

—Bill Peterson, Florida State football coach

"I've had a divorce, heart attack, and world championship all in one year—and I enjoyed them all."

—John Bach, Chicago Bulls assistant coach

"One year we had 17 home runs the entire season. We threw a party when we hit the wall in batting practice."

—Jimmy Snyder, Seattle Mariners interim manager,
on a minor-league squad he once managed

"Being in politics is like being a football coach. You have to be smart enough to know the game and stupid enough to think it is important."

—Eugene McCarthy, U.S. Senator and 1968 Democratic
presidential candidate

"The Yankees are only interested in one thing, and I don't know what that is."

—Outfielder Luis Polonia, criticizing his former team for using him mostly as a pinch-hitter and DH

"I say this will enable me to finish my book. And people say, 'I didn't know you were writing a book.' 'I'm not. I'm reading one.'"

—Jud Heathcote, Michigan State basketball coach, on his retirement